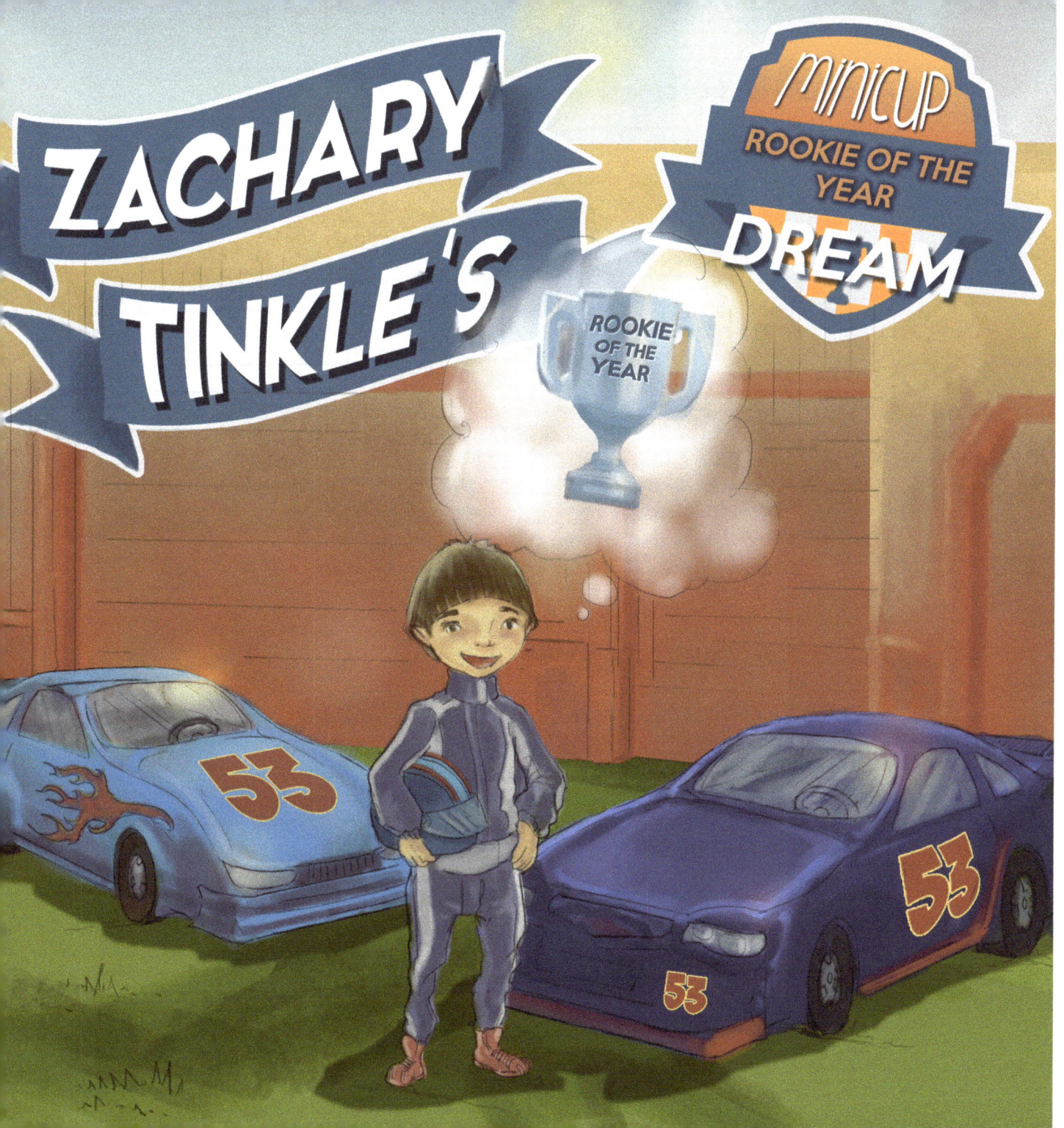

Advanced Book Reviews

"This is a short story of a young boy living out his dream of becoming a NASCAR race car driver, one goal at a time. My favorite part of the book was how Zachary described getting into his race car, suiting up for practice, and his first time on the track. I could almost feel how he felt. I liked the fact that he was going through very tough times at the track. In his words, disasters, and through his persistence, patience and love of the sport he was able to rise above it all, and continue toward his goals.

Zachary doesn't take full credit for his success. He shares it with his family and friends. This, along with hard work, good attitude, and ability to have fun has helped Zachary in reaching his goals. Becoming Rookie Of The Year fulfills another goal and brings him one step closer to his destiny of becoming a NASCAR racer, and giving that President a helicopter ride to his first Daytona 500. This book shows first hand that setting goals, sticking to them, and never giving up, is the fast track to the top. I recommend reading Zachary Tinkle's Mini Cup Rookie Of The Year Dream."
— Steve Naples & Pat Gremo of Central States Region Super Cups

"As a coach for young aspiring racers, this book is something that I have been needing to give to my students for a long time! The author, Zachary Tinkle, who is actually a young aspiring racer himself does an amazing job of showing us how to overcome the ups and downs of getting into this competitive sport. Racing is like no other sport out there, and it has a lot to do with making sure you have the right equipment in place, but most of all the right attitude. Thank you Zachary for being a great example to all kids and to all young racers. I will reccomend this book to all my students!"
- Annamarie Malfitana-Strawhand, Motorsports Marketing Coach and Driving Career Mentor, Marketing At Full Speed

Advanced Book Reviews

"I loved the book! It is very interesting to me to see the "other" side of racing..... all the things that can happen to the racer that might become a DISASTER!"
— Susan Deery, Rockford Speedway

"This book has a good outlook of what it's truly like for a racer and his or her team. You have to 'stick with it' through everything to accomplish your goals. Zachary's story encourages anyone with a goal to never give up."
— Glen Myers, Mazon Speed Bowl & Grundy County Speedway Hall of Fame

---

"This is a must-read for all kids who are pursuing a dream. When all things seem to be falling apart and disaster looms, hang tough and persevere. Reading of Zachary's start in automobile racing, facing the daunting challenges of a new adventure and conquering against a lot of odds will be an inspiration for children in all walks of life. I am waiting for the next chapter!"
— Terry McGraw, motorsports photographer and author of Shutter Speed Reads blog

---

"This book is for everyone that has a dream. It inspires people to not only dream the dream, but live it and experience it fully through thick and thin."
— James L. Ambruoso 'JimmyA' of Finish Line Photos /
Rockford Speedway Photographer / NASCAR Ambassador

Text and illustrations copyright © 2017 Left Paw Press

All rights reserved. No part of this book may be reproduced or transmitted in any form or by any means, electronic or mechanical, including photocopying, recording, or by an information storage retrieval system, without express written permission from the publisher.

No patent liability is assumed with respect to the use of information contained herein. Although every precaution has been taken in the preparation of this book, the publisher and author assume no responsibility for errors or omissions nor is any liability assumed for damages resulting from the use of the information contained herein.

All terms mentioned in this book that are known to be trademarks or service marks have been appropriately capitalized. Left Paw Press cannot attest to the accuracy of this information. Use of a term in this book should not be regarded as affecting the validity of any trademark or service mark.

Every effort has been made to make this book as complete and as accurate as possible, but no warranty or fitness is implied. The information provided is on an "as is" basis. The author and the publisher shall have neither liability nor responsibility to any person or entity with respect to any loss or damages arising from the information contained in this book.

Left Paw Press, publishing imprint of Lauren Originals, Inc.

ISBN: 978-1-943356-33-1

Library of Congress Control Number: 2016961073

PRINTED IN THE UNITED STATES OF AMERICA

Author: Zachary Tinkle

Illustrations: Antonio J. "Nunoh" Díaz

Published and distributed by Left Paw Press, publishing imprint of Lauren Originals, Inc. For educational, corporate, or retail sales accounts, email: info@LeftPawPress.com. For information, address: Left Paw Press 8926 N Greenwood Avenue #293 Niles, IL 60714. Left Paw Press can be found on the web at www.leftpawpress.com.

My car needed to be customized for me. We took it to a guy that made adjustments to the pedals, belts, and seat. I FINALLY got to sit in my car. I loved getting in through the roof, sliding down the seat, and putting my hands on the steering wheel. I gave it two thumbs up! We had to leave the car with him so he could finish the work.

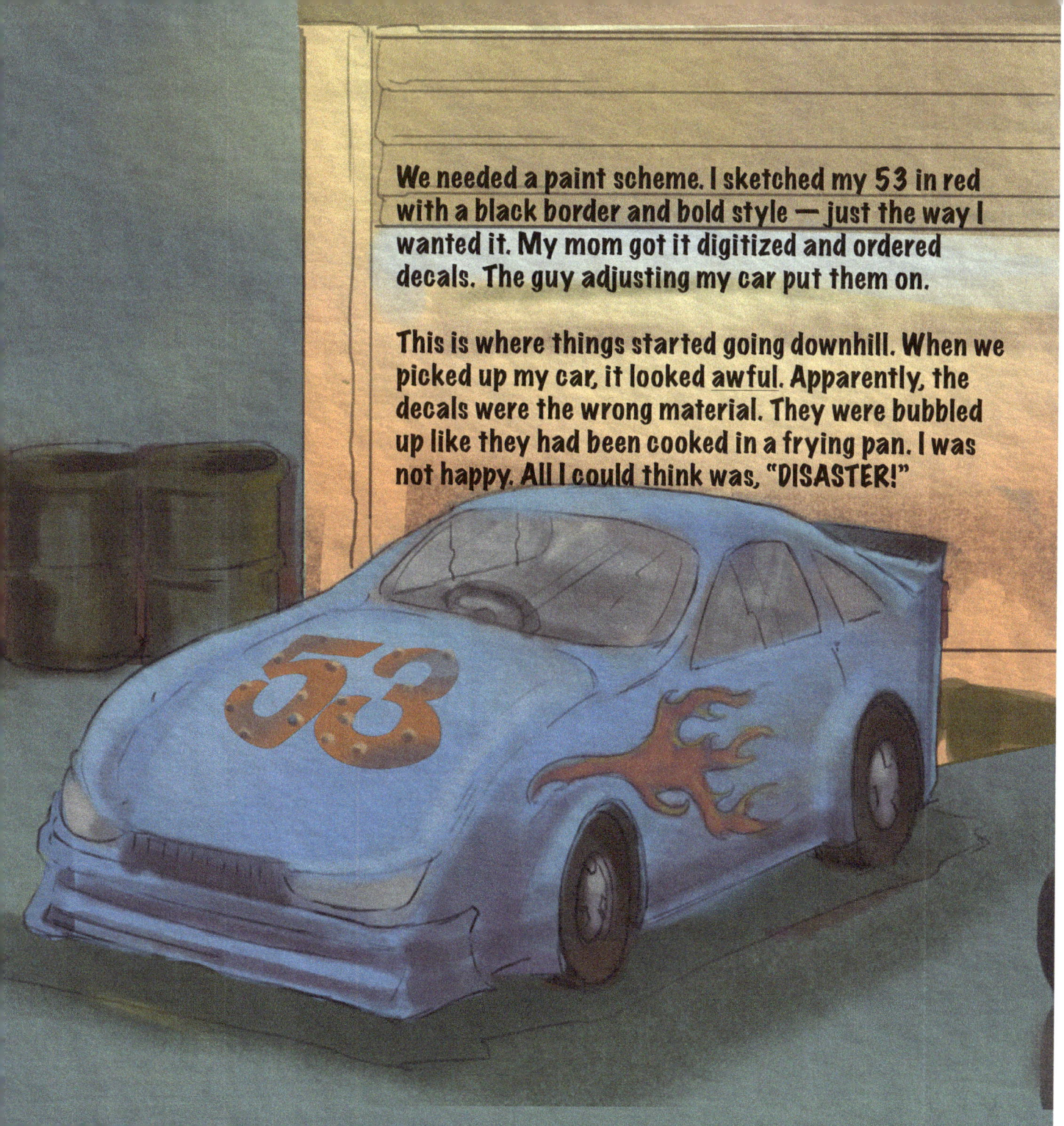

We needed a paint scheme. I sketched my 53 in red with a black border and bold style — just the way I wanted it. My mom got it digitized and ordered decals. The guy adjusting my car put them on.

This is where things started going downhill. When we picked up my car, it looked awful. Apparently, the decals were the wrong material. They were bubbled up like they had been cooked in a frying pan. I was not happy. All I could think was, "DISASTER!"

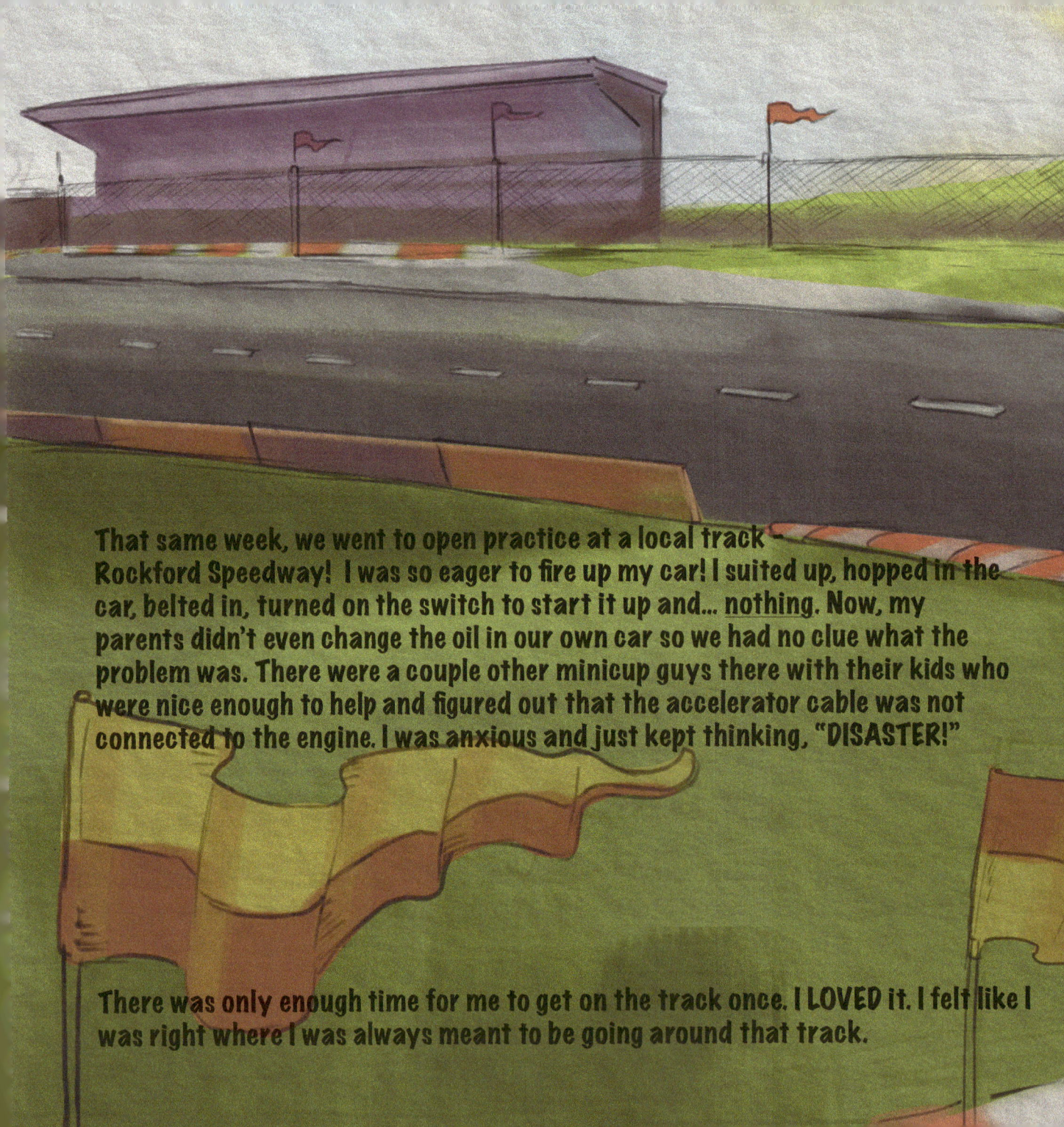

That same week, we went to open practice at a local track - Rockford Speedway! I was so eager to fire up my car! I suited up, hopped in the car, belted in, turned on the switch to start it up and... nothing. Now, my parents didn't even change the oil in our own car so we had no clue what the problem was. There were a couple other minicup guys there with their kids who were nice enough to help and figured out that the accelerator cable was not connected to the engine. I was anxious and just kept thinking, "DISASTER!"

There was only enough time for me to get on the track once. I LOVED it. I felt like I was right where I was always meant to be going around that track.

Our first group practice was at another local track, Grundy County Speedway. The pits are gravel – the kind that flies around in the air and sticks to your skin and everything. It was so fun to start up the engine and get on that track with the other racers for the first time. I thought, "Here I am. I'm a REAL race car driver!"

Not too long after being on the track, I could tell something wasn't right with the car and pulled into my pit. A guy in the league came over and told my dad that he was positive I blew the clutch. He told him how to fix it.

My dad then says to the guy, "Excuse me, I know you've helped me quite a bit already and I appreciate it, but would you mind pointing out what the clutch is?"

I just sat in the trailer thinking, "What a DISASTER!"

Soon, it was time for our first race at a track that took us half a day to get to. It was a long and hot day, but I was thrilled to finally be racing on a real asphalt track.

Practice went ok. I started in the back of the race since I was a rookie. When I went onto the track, my dad came on the radio and asked me if I was ready. I said "I was born ready, baby!"

Things were going ok. I was staying on the lead lap when a car pinched me down around turn three running me off the track — headed for a concrete wall in the infield. My mom stopped videoing and my dad started running down from the spotters' stand. Do you know what they were thinking? "DISASTER!"

That's when they heard the announcer say, "Zachary Tinkle holds his own and gets back on the track!" I had held onto my car for dear life, went through the grass, and got back in the race. It felt great because I had gotten in the race and finished.

It was no secret that three of us racers were really gunning for the title of Rookie of the Year.

I was completely deflated when my dad had to go out of town for two races. This meant my mom was taking me to the races by herself. This really did feel like DISASTER! My mom knew even less about cars than my dad!

The guy that was bound to win the championship and his dad took me aside when they could see that I was feeling defeated. They told me that being Rookie of the Year in this league doesn't just depend on points.

Points matter so I should always do my best, but participation like showing up to every race and a positive attitude counted too. This gave me a little bit of hope... plus, my mom wasn't a total disaster at the two tracks!

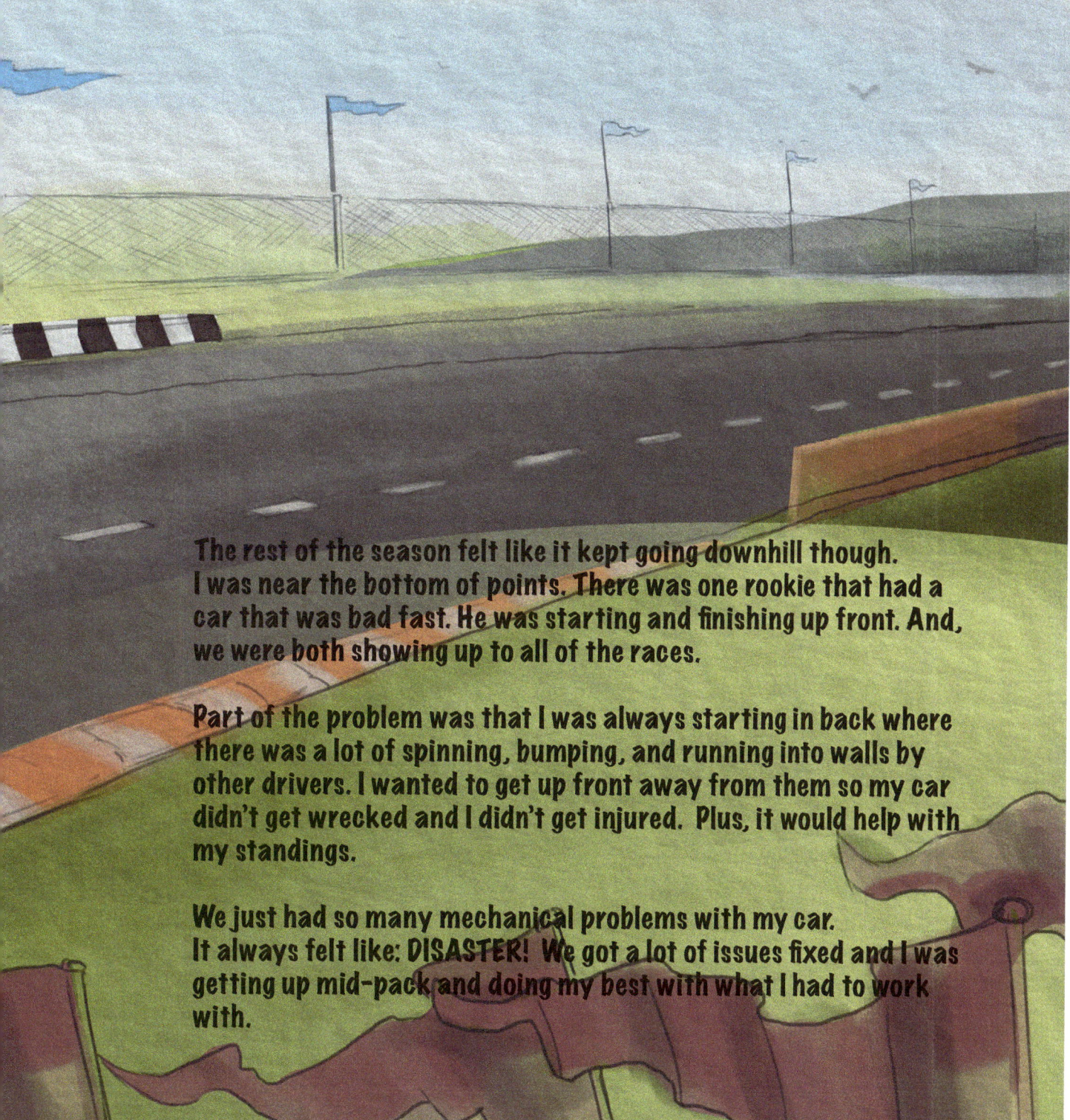

The rest of the season felt like it kept going downhill though. I was near the bottom of points. There was one rookie that had a car that was bad fast. He was starting and finishing up front. And, we were both showing up to all of the races.

Part of the problem was that I was always starting in back where there was a lot of spinning, bumping, and running into walls by other drivers. I wanted to get up front away from them so my car didn't get wrecked and I didn't get injured. Plus, it would help with my standings.

We just had so many mechanical problems with my car. It always felt like: DISASTER! We got a lot of issues fixed and I was getting up mid-pack and doing my best with what I had to work with.

They wanted me to race in a competitive car to see how I could perform. Dad was able to learn the car instead of fixing things all the time.

I started getting Top 5 finishes and even came within eight one-thousandths of a second of winning a race against one of the most experienced drivers in the league.

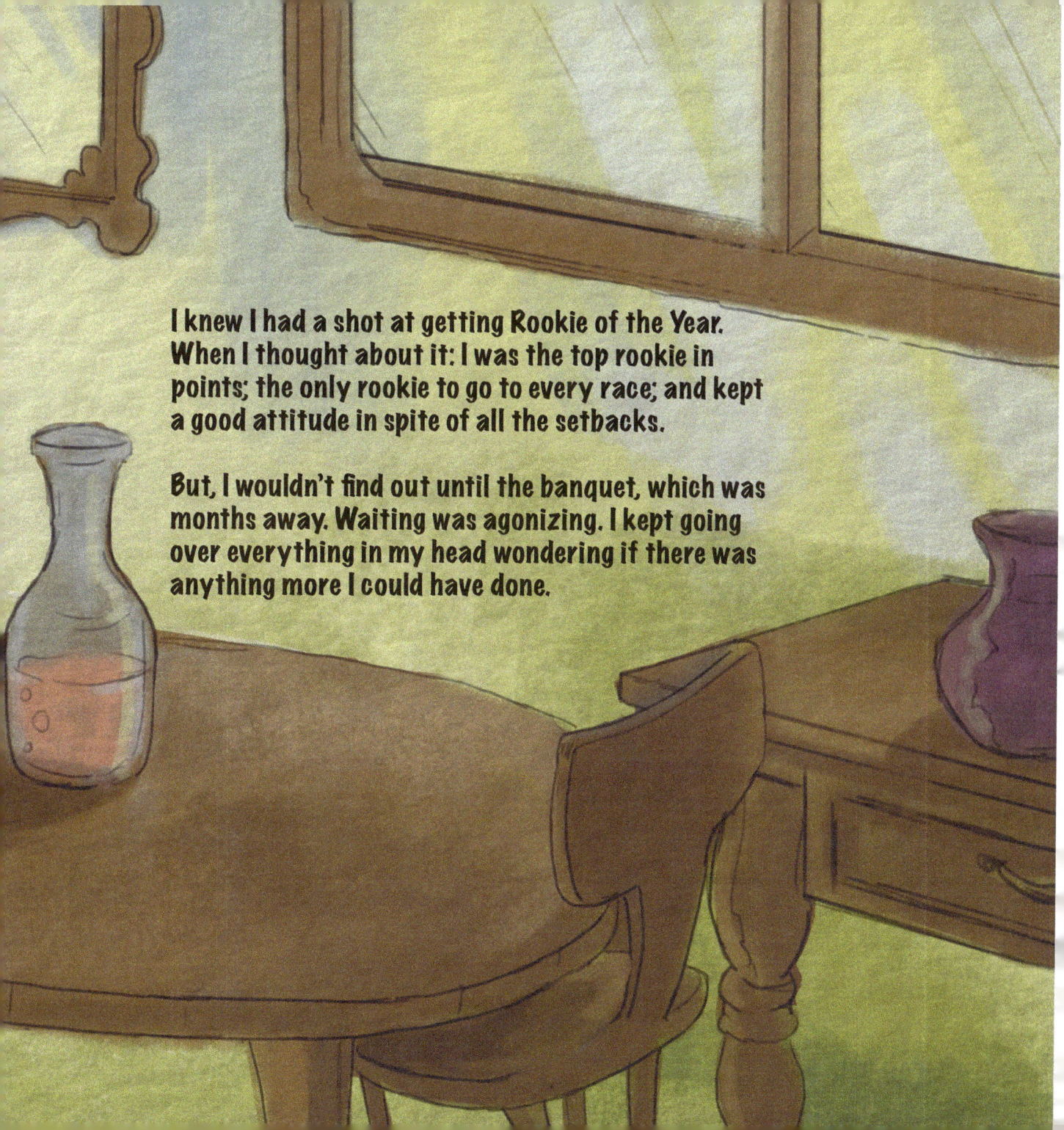

I knew I had a shot at getting Rookie of the Year. When I thought about it: I was the top rookie in points; the only rookie to go to every race; and kept a good attitude in spite of all the setbacks.

But, I wouldn't find out until the banquet, which was months away. Waiting was agonizing. I kept going over everything in my head wondering if there was anything more I could have done.

Banquet day finally came. We ate. The president of the league started his presentation.

Everyone accepted their trophies for how they placed in the series. I even got a big trophy for coming in 5th in championship points.

More talk.

More talk.

Photos.

Speeches.

Zachary Tinkle's MiniCup Decision

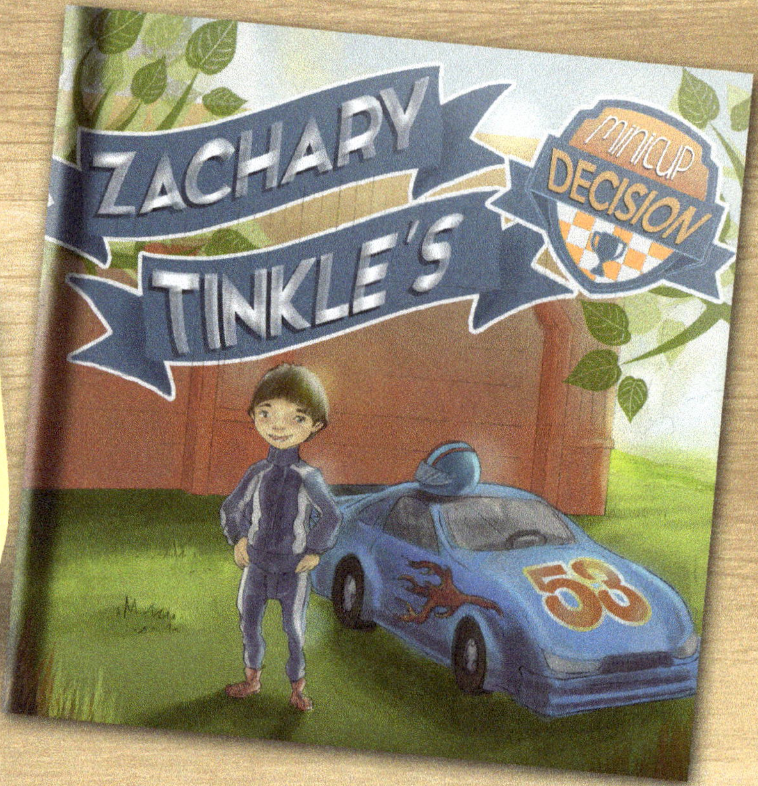

Zachary Tinkle wants to be a NASCAR® driver when he grows up, so he's been practicing with go-karts, getting ready for his first time racing outdoors. But when his parents take him to get the autograph of a famous NASCAR® driver, he sees something he can't believe: A little NASCAR® stock car-just his size. It's a minicup, a half-size stock car that can go 100 miles per hour on the track. Then he meets a father and his young son-who races a mincup! Zachary loves go-karts, but he knows a mincup will get him to the NASCAR big leagues. It's time to make a decision, and talk to Mom and Dad... Children and race fans will love this account by Zachary Tinkle, based on his own true-life story. It's about working hard for your dreams, and the value of thinking through important decisions.

TAMBIÉN EN ESPAÑOL

www.LeftPawPress.com

About the Author

Zachary Tinkle is a 14-year-old stock car driving sensation based in Park Ridge, Illinois who currently races the #53 ½ size minicup car (also known as a super cup car). He will have a full time minicup schedule in 2017 while participating in a late model driver development program with intentions to run a full time late model schedule in 2018.

He is the 2016 Rockford Speedway Wild Wednesday Super Cup Champion. Tinkle is the 2015 Illinois Super Cup State Champion for the Short Track Auto Racing Series (STARS) and 2015 Rockford Speedway National Short Track Champion for Super Cups. Rockford Speedway awarded him the "Lead, Follow, or Get Out Of My Way" award for his 2015 season. He was named the 2015 Most Improved Driver and 2014 Rookie of the Year for Central States Region (CSR) Super Cups.

He has family ties to the Indianapolis, IN and Richmond, IN areas and was born in Cincinnati, OH.

Zachary has aspirations of racing at the top levels of stock car racing including getting a ride with a NASCAR® team.

www.ZacharyTinkle.com.

Photo courtesy Rockford Speedway Photographer / NASCAR Ambassador, James L. Ambruoso 'JimmyA' of Finish Line Photos www.myfinishlinephotos.com

Get the most comprehensive dog fashion illustrations set along with design considerations in the Dog Breeds Pet Fashion Illustration Encyclopedia book set. Includes all of the AKC breeds separated by the seven breed groups.

Coming 2017!

www.PetFashionProfessionals.com

PROUDLY PUBLISHES MEDICAL BOOKS BY
DR. BRAD T TINKLE

www.LeftPawPress.com

RELIEVE STRESS BY COLORING

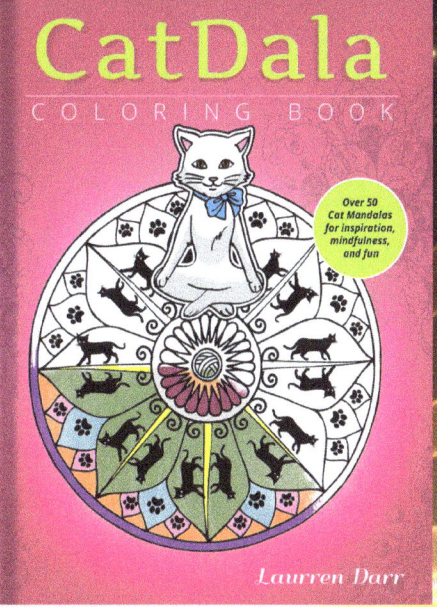

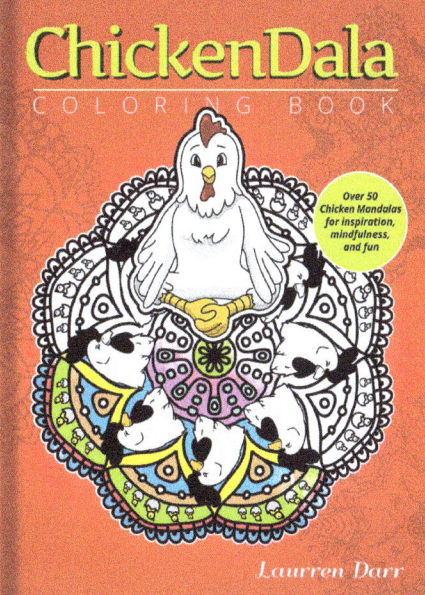

Keep checking LeftPawPress.com for even more pet-related mandala coloring books.

Featured In:

Become a PET FASHION PROFESSIONAL JUMPSTART MEMBER Completely FREE!

The JumpStart Membership swag bag includes: advance notices on our exclusive events, weekly Pet Fashion Trend Updates, access to our Hangouts On Air, our Pet Fashion Professional Badge, AND our "Pet Biz Trade Show Marketing Secrets Unleashed" report!

- Pet Fashion Trends Updates Newsletter
- Pet Fashion Hangouts On Air
- Pet Fashion Professional Membership Badge
- Pet Biz Trade Show Marketing Secrets Unleashed eBook

GET YOUR SWAG BAG NOW!

WWW.PETFASHIONPROFESSIONALS.COM

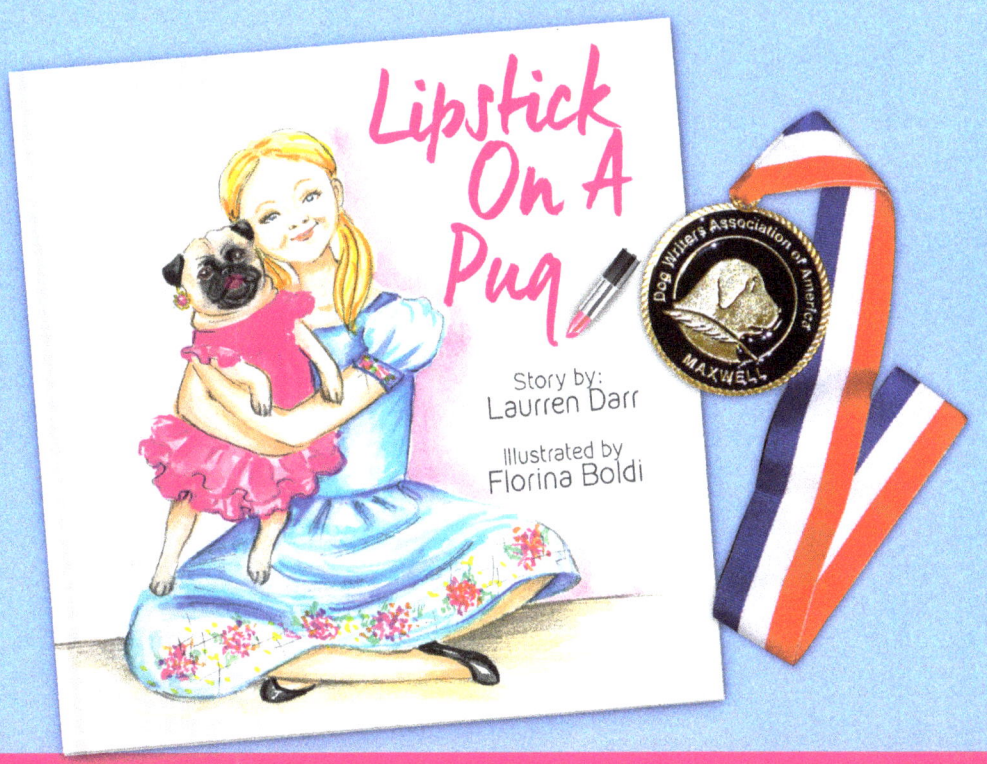

Learn about the roots of Laurren's plumb pug craziness and obsession with pet fashion in this children's book that will teach about the love of dog, pet rescue, and the unbreakable bonds between humans and their pets.

Lipstick On A Pug won the 2015 Children's Book of the Year Maxwell Medallion from the Dog Writers Association of America.

Also available in coloring book format

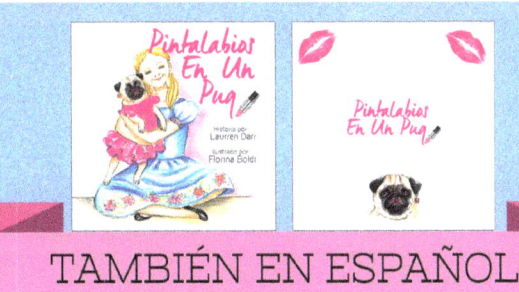

TAMBIÉN EN ESPAÑOL

PET FASHION BOOKS
AVAILABLE FROM LEFT PAW PRESS
Lipstick On A Pug
Story by: Laurren Darr
Illustrated by Florina Boldi
DOG BREEDS PET FASHION ILLUSTRATION ENCYCLOPEDIA
VOL 1
TOY BREEDS
VOL 2
NON-SPORTING BREEDS
VOL 3
TERRIER BREEDS
Pet Fashion 2014 ALMANAC
Pet Fashion 2015 ALMANAC
Pet Fashion 2016 ALMANAC
LEFT PAW Press
www.LeftPawPress.com

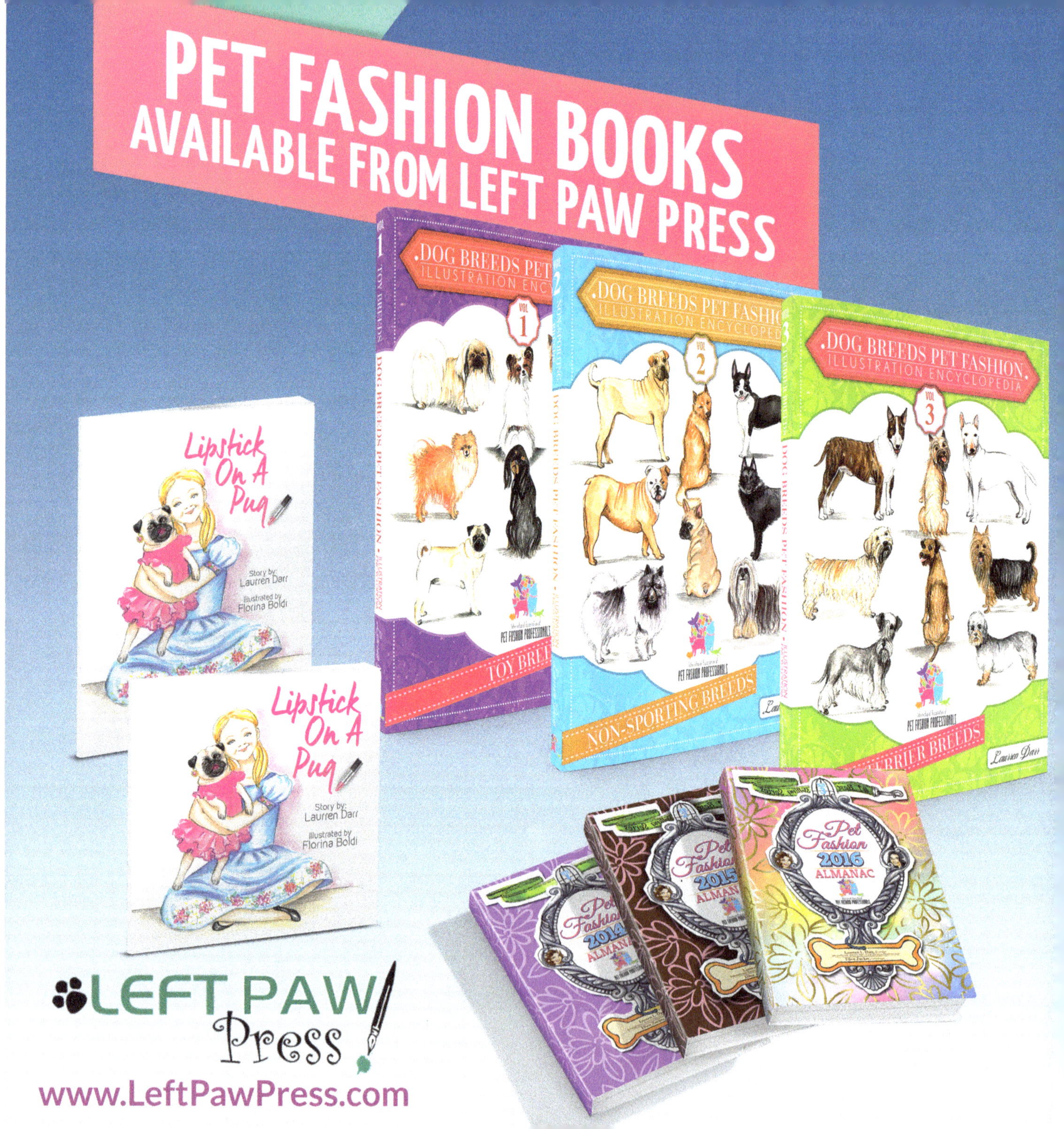

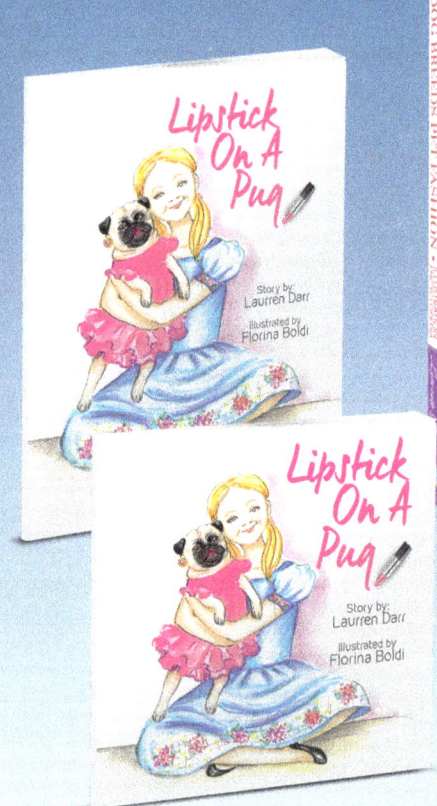

www.ingramcontent.com/pod-product-compliance
Lightning Source LLC
Chambersburg PA
CBHW060948170426
43201CB00023B/2420